PUBERTY:

AN
ILLUSTRATED MANUAL
FOR
PARENTS AND DAUGHTERS

PUBERTY:

AN
ILLUSTRATED MANUAL
FOR
PARENTS AND DAUGHTERS

ANGELA HYNES
Illustrated by Gita Lloyd

TOR ®

A Tom Doherty Associates Book
New York

PUBERTY: AN ILLUSTRATED MANUAL FOR PARENTS
AND DAUGHTERS

A TOR BOOK
Published by Tom Doherty Associates, Inc.
49 West 24 Street
New York, NY 10010

Illustrated by Gita Lloyd

First edition: May 1989
0 9 8 7 6 5 4 3 2 1

Contents

A Note of Explanation

In times past, the kind of information that is in this book would have been passed on from generation to generation in the traditional "mother/daughter talk." But today we cannot take for granted that a girl is living with both parents. With a divorce rate running at 50 percent it is entirely possible that the task of answering questions about puberty and related topics will fall to a grandmother, aunt, older sister, stepmother, or family friend.

Similarly, even if a girl lives in a two-parent home, we cannot be sure that those parents assume traditional roles. Perhaps a girl's father will be the one to tell her the facts of life.

For the sake of clarity and convenience, throughout the text we have referred to the girl as your "daughter." No matter what your actual relationship, the information and assistance contained in this book are still valid. However, when you read the stories in Chapter Nine, you may wish to make some substitutions in the relationships between the child and the adults to make it seem more relevant to the young woman you're talking to.

CHAPTER ONE

Talking to
Your Daughter

From the moment we are born to the moment we die, our bodies are in a constant state of change. But at puberty the human body undergoes more noticeable and more sudden changes than at any other time.

For girls, beginning to menstruate is the most significant happening of puberty, and the one that to most people indicates a passage into adulthood. It comes, however, as part and parcel of a number of other events that occur over a period of several years.

These changes, which generally get under way somewhere between the ages of eight and ten, include a growth spurt, a widening of the pelvis, an increase in body fat, the development of breasts, the growth of body hair, and changes in skin and hair condition.

This process of change from a child's body to an adult's coincides with a time of great psychological and social upheaval. You probably remember only too well how the adolescent years can be joy-filled, but also traumatic. Your daughter is seeking to establish her own identity, but she is also at the mercy of new and tumultuous emotional and sexual feelings.

The pressures on young people today are well publicized. If, as parents, you can help your children, in a straightforward yet compassionate way, handle the *physical* side of becoming an adult, you can eliminate one possible area of stress.

Experts believe that preteens who enter puberty with a clear understanding of what is happening to them have a much easier time of it than those who are ignorant or confused. Also, a young person who is comfortable with his or her body is more likely to have the self-confidence to handle the problems of adolescence.

Children need help. Hearing about teenage lifestyles that encompass sex, pregnancy, drugs, alcohol, and dropping out of school, many parents tend to assume that their children are more sophisticated than they really are. How often have you joked that your kids know more about the world than you do?

After all, many topics that we only whispered about when we were adolescents are now displayed in the media. You only have to open a women's magazine to see advertisements for tampons, and there are commercials for douches and condoms on network television. Radio and television talk shows often explore intimate subjects.

But the fact that kids are getting into all kinds of trouble indicates that they don't know it all. You cannot rely on sex education classes, which are usually offered too late, when children are already well into puberty, the mass media, or her friends to provide your daughter with information about puberty. She needs to hear the true facts from someone she trusts and with whom she feels comfortable. This means you—the responsible adult in her life.

In an ideal situation, you will have been answering your daughter's questions throughout her life. Children are generally fascinated by their own bodies, and usually offer adults plenty of opportunities to talk about them. But don't worry if those opportunities have not arisen, or if you have let them pass by because of your own discomfort with the subject. You can easily play catch-up, and the best time to do it is before your daughter enters puberty.

This doesn't mean that you have to sit down behind closed doors for the proverbial "parent/daughter talk." Wherever you can create a cozy feeling between you and your child is a good place to bring intimate subjects into the open. Sometimes literally going "out in the open" works well: walking on the beach, sharing a picnic lunch, taking a drive. Listen to how these parents have dealt with the matter:

> "Chrissie, my twelve-year-old, and I have gotten into the habit of taking our two terriers for a walk every evening, just before Chrissie's bedtime. Being out of the house and walking in the semidarkness seems to make her very comfortable. We've talked

· 3 ·

about all kinds of intimate subjects, and if something comes up during the day that bothers her, she knows we'll have time together that night to discuss it."

"I have two girls, eight and ten. About once a month we have a 'girls' night out.' I avoid places like the movies, where you can't talk. We usually go shopping at the mall or to a museum—something like that. Then I take them to a nice restaurant for dinner. We chatter nonstop about everything under the sun, and we've covered all the facts of life this way! Often the girls bring up the subject themselves."

Even after you've picked your time and place to talk, or an ideal opportunity has spontaneously arisen, it's often difficult to find the right words. One of the easiest ways to start is by sharing some anecdotes about your own history. You can talk about your parents' attitudes, how you got your sex education, your first experiences with puberty and sex, and your feelings about everything.

While you want to let your children know that you empathize with them, it's better not to tell stories that are frightening or embarrassing. Telling your daughter how cramps prevented you from enjoying your junior prom, or how your sister started her period while playing softball and got stains on her clothes, is not reassuring!

Focus on how you dealt with situations as they arose. When you got your period at school did you go to the nurse or the principal's secretary for a pad? Did you buy one from a machine in the bathroom? Did you tell your teacher or best friend about it? Did you call home and ask your mom what to do?

When you wanted to start wearing a bra did you talk to your mother about it, ask an older sister or trusted aunt for help, or save your allowance to buy one yourself?

Another good way to get the conversation rolling is to comment on something you've read or heard, whether it's a statistic or a television show. Often this objective discussion will easily turn into a personal one. Offer the child plenty of opportunities to ask questions, and answer her simply and honestly.

Remember that the attitudes you instill in your daughter at this point will color her feelings about her body for the rest of her life. If you represent menstruation as something painful and embarrassing, to be dreaded every month, that is how she will probably experience it. On the other hand, if you explain that her periods are a sign that her body is healthy and functioning as it should, her view will be much more positive.

It's possible that your daughter might already have picked up some negative views on the subject from school friends, or even from you in an unguarded moment! You can counteract this by explaining how much things have changed in the last few years. There is medication that can control menstrual cramping and eliminate other physical and emotional effects of menstruation. Also, napkins and tampons become much more convenient and effective every year.

Most important, when talking to your daughter, try to avoid using euphemisms like "the monthlies," or negative phrases such as "the curse." By using the biologically correct words for body parts and functions, you can take much of the mystique out of the subject. Some of these words are tongue twisters, so there is a pronunciation guide at the end of the book to smooth your way.

CHAPTER TWO

What and When Is "Normal"?

Puberty is defined as the period of time during which a child's body takes on the characteristics of an adult body and becomes capable of reproduction.

The process usually happens over three to five years and, for girls, between the ages of eight and seventeen. "Usually" is the all-important word here. Every individual is on a different time-table. One girl might start getting breast buds at eight and pubic hair at ten; another might not see those changes until she is twelve and fourteen. Yet both girls are perfectly normal.

Being "normal," just like the rest of the crowd, is of vital importance to the preteen and teenager. At no other time in life is peer acceptance so important. Adolescents want to look, act, and be just like their friends. This is when you will hear yourself trotting out that old saw, "If Sharon jumped off a cliff, would you jump, too?"

Many young girls go through a great deal of anguish because they are the last—or first—in their crowd to get breasts or start their periods. They talk of being made fun of, or of provoking jealousy. They feel different, like "freaks"—exactly what they fear most!

"I dread taking a shower after gym class because everyone else is still flat-chested and I've already started developing. I hardly go to the beach any more because I think everyone is staring at me. When my folks make me go with them, I keep my T-shirt on over my bathing suit."

Linda, age nine

"I'm the only girl in my class who hasn't had a period yet. All the kids were teasing me; some of them even said there must be something wrong with me. So I started lying and saying that I've started. I hope I start soon because I feel bad about it."

Jennifer, age fourteen

Your daughter needs to be reassured that regardless of when her physical development starts, within a few years she and her friends will all end up in the same place: grown women who have reached their full potential. Slow starters often develop more quickly and so catch up with their friends. Almost everyone knows at least one girl who went away for the summer as a skinny little tomboy and came back that fall looking like a woman.

Often during this time, there is a shuffling and regrouping of friendships. The girls who have matured more quickly band together. They become appearance-conscious, experimenting with makeup and clothes and talking about boys. The girl who is chronologically the same age but younger in physical terms, and therefore socially younger, can be ostracized from the group. If your daughter is in this position, encourage her to pursue ac-

tivities she likes, and through them to make new friends with girls who are in a similar stage of development.

> "I felt so bad for Tracy last year. Her two best friends, who were also twelve, started strutting around in fancy clothes and lots of frills. Tracy was way behind them in terms of physical development and just wasn't ready for all that. She felt really left out, but also didn't really want to be like them. She had always been at home in the water, so at her school open house I talked to the gym teacher, who agreed to let Tracy try out for the swim team. She made the team, and now she has a new group of friends. All they talk about is lap times and turn techniques. Tracy's much happier."
>
> Tracy's mother

It is very important that a girl develops a high level of self-esteem and a positive attitude about her body. If she is early or slow in developing, try not to tease her. Talk to your partner or her siblings if they are bent on making fun of her. Ask them to have some compassion for her feelings. What can seem like harmless fun to the rest of the family can be torture to an insecure girl.

Compliment her on her appearance, focusing on her good points. Insincere flattery is easily detected. If she has pretty hair or good skin, tell her. When she looks particularly attractive in a certain outfit or color, let her know. Praise her accomplishments and good qualities. Celebrate good report cards, and don't let acts of kindness or generosity go unnoticed. This type of positive reinforcement goes a long way toward establishing feelings of self-worth.

Because heredity is the most important influence on the onset of puberty, it will help if you recall your own timetable. If you were a late starter, your daughter is likely to be one. If you started early, so may she. Tell her about your own experiences and compare notes. Older sisters, aunts, and grandmothers on both sides of the family can also be consulted about how old they were when they developed breasts and started their periods.

Although the puberty time clock is largely genetically controlled, there are a few other factors that can influence when a girl begins to menstruate:

- Poor Nutrition. If a girl consistently eats a diet deficient in the basic nutrients, her first period may be delayed. This is not very common in most Western cultures.

- Body Fat. An obese child might start her periods early. Research indicates that the female body needs to be at a certain "critical mass" in order to menstruate. Generally, a woman will menstruate if at least twenty percent of her body weight is composed of fat. This is nature's way of being sure that a woman has the fat necessary to carry and nourish a baby.

There is a flip side to this coin. Girls who have a low percentage of body fat—usually because they are very athletic—often start having periods late, because their bodies are below that critical level. If your daughter is a budding gymnast, track star, or dancer and is very slim, don't be surprised if she starts menstruating a year or so later than you would have anticipated.

Young girls who are anorexic (starve themselves) can also delay puberty. This is a serious condition that needs the intervention of a physician and probably a psychotherapist.

- Ill Health. A child with diabetes or who contracts a severe illness during puberty may have a delayed start to menstruation.

• Severe Stress. A girl who undergoes emotional trauma, such as the loss of a parent, or some other stress-causing event, can be a late starter.

• Geographic Considerations. Girls living at very high altitudes sometimes begin their periods later than girls living at lower altitudes. But other factors, such as climate or race, have no bearing on menstruation.

The only times you should worry about your daughter's development are if she shows signs of advanced maturation before the age of eight, or no signs of adult characteristics by the age of fifteen. In these instances, she may have a hormonal imbalance that needs medical attention.

CHAPTER THREE

Signs of Puberty

As your daughter begins puberty, you and she will see a number of outward signs of maturation.

Growth Spurt

This is an early sign of puberty. Up to the age of two, babies grow quickly. Then, between two and the onset of puberty, children grow at a rate of roughly two inches per year. During the first year or two of puberty, that rate of growth increases, sometimes almost doubling. You'll notice your children suddenly "shooting up" and outgrowing their clothes.

Sometimes children's feet and hands grow first; then the rest of their body catches up. If this happens, children often go through a clumsy phase. They will sleep long hours and be difficult to rouse. They will probably eat more than they did formerly. Be patient with them through this fairly short-lived awkward stage. It may seem to you as if your children's bodies are a little out of control—sometimes it feels that way to them, too.

"I couldn't believe it, I suddenly had Minnie Mouse feet! I could wear my mom's shoes. I was tripping over everything and felt like a real klutz. But then the rest of me caught up, and now my feet seem normal."

Nancy, age eleven

Girls start their growth spurt a good two years before boys. The average eleven-year-old girl is usually taller than a boy of the same age. If your daughter worries about towering over the boys, reassure her that boys generally catch up with and over-take girls by their mid- to late teens. For girls, the growth spurt is usually over by the time they start menstruating. Most girls don't grow more than another couple of inches after their periods start. Heredity will give a good clue to your child's eventual height.

Body Shape

As the body grows taller during puberty, it also "fills out." In girls, the pelvic bones grow and widen, making their waists look smaller.

There is a simultaneous increase in body fat, especially around the hips and thighs. All of these changes, which result in a more rounded, "womanly" figure, occur in anticipation of the girl's child-bearing years. Just how curvy or slender a girl eventually will be depends on genes—a glance at female blood relatives on both sides of the family will provide clues.

There can be a danger of confusing this weight gain during

puberty with general obesity. We live in a society so obsessed with being slim that the sudden fleshing out of your daughter's thighs might send her into a mild panic. Your adolescent daughter may be very vulnerable to the cult of slimness and the social prejudice against overweight women. It is well documented that many seventh- and eighth-graders are preoccupied with dieting to the detriment of good nutrition—not to mention the detriment of their emotional well-being.

Furthermore, serious (sometimes fatal) eating disorders such as anorexia and bulimia are on the increase, particularly among adolescent girls. You can do much to avoid the pains of both adolescent obesity and eating disorders by establishing sound nutritional principles and an exercise regimen for your young children. It's almost inevitable that preteens and teens are going to eat junk food when they're out without their parents, but you can counteract that pattern by providing healthy meals at home.

Body Hair

Around the time her breast buds are developing, your daughter will probably also start seeing the first pubic hairs growing on her vulva, the fleshy outer lips of the vagina. Initially, the hairs will be sparse, downy, and not very curly. Over the next few years they will become thicker, coarser, and curlier.

About one year after a girl begins menstruating, the growth of her pubic hair will be complete. Generally, pubic hair grows in a neat triangular formation with a straight top. But it is not at all unusual for a woman to have a little hair trailing up toward her navel, and growing down the top of her thighs.

One myth that should be dispelled is that pubic hair is always the same color as the hair on your head. There can be quite a difference, just as some men's beards are a different color from their scalp hair.

Underarm hair starts to appear after pubic hair has been growing for about a year. Around the same time, the hair on her arms and legs will darken and thicken.

As she becomes hypersensitive about her appearance, your daughter will probably want to start experimenting with hair-removal techniques: you undoubtedly will think she's too young, but the two of you should discuss her options. Make sure that she knows that hair removal is a matter of personal choice, not a requirement of adulthood. But if she decides to go ahead and remove underarm or leg hair, be sensitive to her feelings.

"I have almost-black hair. Suddenly last year I started to get really thick, dark hair on my legs. The guys at school used to make gorilla noises when I walked by. I told my mom I was going to shave my legs, but she said no. She comes from a

culture where they don't care about that. I just
went ahead and did it when I was sleeping over at
my friend's. At first my mom was really mad, but
now I think she's used to it."

Annamarie, age thirteen

The most popular methods of hair removal or of decreasing
its obviousness are:

• Shaving. It's a myth that shaving causes hair to
grow back thicker and darker. Sometimes hair ap-
pears more coarse because shaving blunts the ends
of the hair shafts, resulting in bristly stubble and
shadow. Shaving is actually the cheapest, fastest,
and most convenient way to remove body hair. The
recommended method is to do it in the shower,
using a sharp, clean razor.

• Waxing. This option is quick, effective, and long
lasting, but it does sting! A salon waxing is probably outside the budget of a young girl's allowance.
Should she decide to use a home kit, supervise her
carefully. Don't allow her to wax her legs if her
skin is sunburned, cut, or irritated.

• Depilatory Creams. These are caustic and work
by eating away the hair at its root. But since skin
and hair are both largely composed of protein, a
cream that is too strong or is left on too long will
start eating away at the skin. Insist that your
daughter follow the manufacturer's instructions to
the letter—especially the one about patch testing
the cream for an allergic reaction twenty-four
hours before using it.

- Bleaching. Bleaching lasts about a month and can be a good solution if the unwanted hair is not too thick or the growth too heavy. Again, hydrogen peroxide is a harsh chemical and the manufacturer's instructions must be followed.

Sometimes a girl will notice hairs around her nipples or a light growth on her upper lip. Neither of these is in any way abnormal. Breast hairs should never be plucked, waxed, or shaved, as infections can result. Bleaching is really the only safe solution.

Upper-lip hair can be dealt with by any of the above solutions, but please make sure the products used are especially formulated for facial application. If your teenager is very upset by her facial hair, assure her that there is another option—electrolysis—which is open to her when she is adult. Although electrolysis is time-consuming, expensive, and uncomfortable, it *is* permanent.

Body Odor

During puberty, the body's sweat glands enlarge and become more active. A girl will notice that she starts to perspire under her arms, on her palms, on the soles of her feet, and around her genitals. She will also notice that her body will develop a new, adult odor if scrupulous hygiene habits are not observed.

Perspiration itself has no odor; it only becomes offensive when it reacts with bacteria on the skin. Clean clothes and daily bathing with soap should be all anyone needs to stay smelling fresh. Suggest that your daughter wear cotton underwear, which does not promote sweating as much as nylon and other synthetic fabrics. Once she enters her teens, she will likely want to start using antiperspirants or deodorants, powders, and perfumes.

Deodorants and antiperspirants are perfectly safe for under-arms, but should never be used around the vulva. The perfumes and chemicals in them can cause irritation. This warning also applies to the "feminine hygiene" sprays that are made especially for that area. Explain to your daughter that the vagina is naturally clean. Around the same time that her sweat glands become more active, it is possible that she will notice a new feeling of wetness in her genital area. Most girls have a clear or milky discharge for several months before they start menstruating. This mucus is perfectly normal. As long as she washes away the daily accumulation of sweat and body secretions, the teen-ager should not have to worry about odor.

However, an unusual odor or heavy vaginal discharge might be signs of a vaginal infection. The best thing to do is see a doctor, not try to mask the condition with perfumes.

Many young girls like to use a perfumed talc or baby powder. This is fine to use around the breasts or under the arms, but again, such products should not be used in the genital area. Habitual talc use has been linked to cervical cancer. The data are as yet inconclusive, but why take chances? A good attitude will set your daughter off on a lifetime of healthy habits.

Hair and Skin

These days, "beauty awareness" starts in girls when they are very young. Preteen and teen magazines, films, and television shows all alert girls to society's attitudes toward makeup and glamour. Just as adolescents become more appearance-conscious, puberty starts playing havoc with their skin and hair.

As the sweat glands mature, so do the oil glands on the scalp, face, upper chest, and back. Hair tends to become lank and greasy. Daily washing will keep this under control, so provide your daughter with a mild shampoo formulated for oily hair. Also, reconcile yourself and the rest of the family to the fact that her bathroom time will increase dramatically!

Skin and skin care are a little more complicated. About four out of five adolescents experience mild breakouts of pimples, or "zits," and are prone to whiteheads and blackheads. Blackheads, incidentally, have nothing to do with dirt. They are collections of oil, bacteria, and dead skin cells that plug the pores and are oxidized (turn black) when exposed to the air. Whiteheads are similar but are under the skin. Pimples are raised inflammations that can become pus-filled and infected.

Once again, raging hormones are the culprit. Even well after puberty, many women continue to break out just before their periods. In the past, chocolate, french fries, or iodine-rich foods were erroneously blamed for acne. But the condition *can* be worsened by an unhealthy lifestyle, and also by stress (hence the pimple that always erupts right before a big date).

Teach your daughter a commonsense approach to dealing with pimples. The most important point is not to perform "bathroom surgery." Pimples should never be squeezed, picked, or pricked—not even with a sterile needle—as these habits can lead to infections and permanent scarring. This especially holds true for blacks, Asians, and dark-skinned Caucasians, as their skin tends to form keloids, which are raised, permanent scars.

There are plenty of good over-the-counter medications designed to aid, control, or cover occasional breakouts. Proper and judicious use of them can help your daughter sit out this usually temporary condition.

A smaller number of adolescents suffer from severe and prolonged acne that covers their faces, backs, and chests with inflamed pustules. This unsightly condition can cause social and emotional problems for years.

"Kids at school really give me a hard time. They call me 'pizza face' and act as though it's my fault, as though I could do something about it if I wanted. All I want to do is crawl into a cave and never come out."

Diane, age thirteen

This type of acne needs medical attention from a dermatologist, a physician who specializes in skin care. Most health insurance plans will cover dermatological care. The doctor can prescribe medications, like tetracycline and Accutane, and topical creams, such as Retin-A, which have excellent results over a period of months. Furthermore, a dermatologist can supervise long-term rehabilitation of the skin, so that the sufferer does not carry the literal and figurative scars of acne for life.

Some minor consolations for your daughter:

• Boys generally tend to suffer more severely than girls from acne as the male hormone androgen (which women have only in small amounts) is largely responsible for the condition.

• Women with excessively oily skin benefit later in life, because their skin ages less quickly and forms fewer lines than that of their dry-skinned friends.

CHAPTER FOUR

Breast Development

Breast development is often—but not always—one of the earliest indicators of puberty. Some girls start to develop breasts when they are as young as eight, but generally this happens between the ages of eleven and thirteen. Everyone develops at her own pace, and neither you nor your daughter should worry if she is a little ahead of or behind her classmates.

The entire process of breast development takes three or four years. In childhood, only the nipples are raised from the chest wall. The first stage of development occurs when the nipple and areola (the circle of darker skin around the nipple) get larger and darker and a little puffier. Gradually, glandular tissue begins to grow under the areola. This is called a breast bud.

Breast buds may feel tender for a while when they are growing, but assure your daughter that this feeling will pass once she has begun to menstruate regularly. Sometimes one breast bud grows before the other, causing the girl to think that something is wrong with her. This is not at all unusual. By forewarning her that breasts can develop asymmetrically, you can defuse her fears.

After budding, breasts continue to grow. First they assume a conelike shape, then gradually become more rounded. Fully grown adult breasts are composed of a glandular mass and fatty

tissue interlaced with milk ducts and a blood supply. The eventual size, shape, elevation, and appearance and position of nipples varies tremendously from woman to woman.

Probably more anxiety has been experienced by more women due to the appearance of their breasts than over any other physical attribute! It's very important that at this early stage you instill in your daughter a sense that her worth does not depend on the size or shape of her body. Point out that there are beautiful, successful women of every figure type. Use your daughter's heroines as examples.

Once your daughter's breasts begin to show appreciable development, the question of whether or not she should wear a bra will arise. It may even arise *before* she shows any appreciable development! Either way, the subject might be embarrassing to her.

"I'm about the only kid in my class who still doesn't wear a bra. I know I'm kind of flat, but even some of the other girls who don't have breasts wear bras. I'd like to get one, but I'm afraid my mom will laugh if I ask her."

Bonnie, age eleven

Let her off the hook by bringing it up yourself. When you notice that her breasts are beginning to develop, or that her friends are wearing bras, simply ask her, "Would you like to start wearing a bra?" To help her make that decision, she should have the facts. Make sure that she knows that, contrary to street lore, wearing a bra will not make her breasts grow quicker or larger, nor will it stop them from sagging later in life.

These days, bras are not mandatory for women, but are a matter of personal choice. Your daughter may want to wear a bra because it feels more comfortable during sports or other activities, she is self-conscious about "jiggling" without one, or her friends are all wearing them. If this is the case, offer to take her to a store where you can help her choose the right size, and where she can try them on.

On the other hand, she might decide that bras are uncomfortable, inconvenient, and unnecessary. The main point is not to tease her, but to be supportive (no pun intended) of her choice.

Most girls start menstruating when their breasts are about three-quarters fully developed. Once your daughter has settled into a regular menstrual cycle, she might start to experience some breast tenderness and swelling prior to the onset of her period. This is due to hormonal shifts, and again, forewarned is forearmed.

This is the best time to teach her how to perform a breast self-examination. The American Cancer Association has extended its efforts to educate women on self-examinations into schools. Breast cancer is not common among young girls, but they should, as early as possible, get into the very important

lifetime habit of self-examination. Additionally, the more familiar a girl is with the look and texture of her breasts, the better
able she will be to detect any changes that might occur.

The exam should be conducted every month during the
week after a woman's period, when her breasts are free from any
swelling caused by premenstrual hormonal activity. For reasons
not fully understood yet by the scientific community, women
who live together in the same house or dormitory often get their
periods at the same time. If you and your daughter are in synch,
consider doing your breast exams together, but only if you both
feel comfortable doing so. In any event, you might want to dem-
onstrate the exam technique on yourself so your daughter can
clearly see how it is done and you can answer any questions she
has.

This is how to do a self-exam as prescribed by the American Cancer Association:

Step 1. Palpation (Lying Down)

To examine your right breast, put a pillow or folded towel under your right shoulder. Place your right hand behind your head. With your left hand, fingers flat, start at the outermost top of your breast and press gently, in circular motions, around an imaginary clockface that covers all of your breast. Gradually move inward until you have examined every inch of your breast, including your nipple. Gently squeeze the nipple between your thumb and forefinger.

Repeat the same procedure on your left breast, using your right hand.

Step 2. Visual Inspection (in Front of a Mirror)

Inspect your breasts with your arms relaxed at your sides. If you're like most women, your left and right breasts won't match exactly.

Next, raise your arms high overhead. Look for any change in the contours of each breast, including swelling, skin dimpling, or change in the nipple.

Then rest your palms on your hips and press down firmly. Again, look for any changes.

You'll gain confidence with each monthly exam. If you notice any change such as a lump, hard knot, or a thickening of the breast tissue or any unusual discharge from the nipple, call your doctor.

CHAPTER FIVE

Sex Organs

During puberty, both the external and internal sex organs mature. Girls begin to develop a fascination with their bodies and become curious about that area between their legs. If a girl hasn't already been instinctively masturbating, she might start now. Unless masturbating becomes a preoccupation or obsession it is a healthy way for a girl to satisfy her curiosity about her body.

It's a good idea to channel that curiosity into healthy exploration that will allow her to become familiar and comfortable with that part of her body. Talking about, touching, and even looking at her pubic area (the last with the help of a hand-held mirror) will help demystify the subject.

External Organs

The genital area, also known as the vulva, is at the junction of a girl's legs. The pad of flesh that covers the pubic bone and on which pubic hair grows is called the mons. About the time hair begins to sprout, the mons becomes fattier and more prominent.

The mons divides into the outer lips—labia majora—of the vulva. They too get fleshier and grow hair during puberty. Between the outer lips is another pair of lips, the labia minora. These inner lips protect the delicate, moist skin of the vaginal opening. At puberty, the inner lips usually become darker in color—changing from pale pink to darker red or an almost-brown hue—and wrinkled-looking. In some girls they are completed enfolded by the outer lips, in others they can protrude outside the outer lips. Often, one side is bigger or longer than the other. All these variations are perfectly normal.

Where the inner lips join at the top lies the clitoris. This is a small bud-shaped bit of tissue that is very sensitive to touch. The clitoris has a lot of nerve endings which send messages to the pleasure centers in the brain. Touching or stimulating the clitoris during masturbation or sexual intercourse can be very pleasurable and can ultimately lead to orgasm.

Below the clitoris and within the inner lips is the urethra. This is the tiny opening through which urine leaves the body.

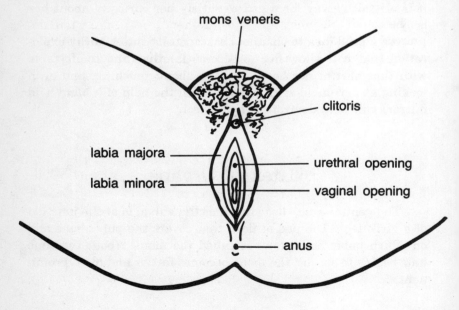

mons veneris

clitoris

labia majora

urethral opening

labia minora

vaginal opening

anus

The urethra becomes more prominent and noticeable during puberty.

Below the urethra, and somewhat larger than it, is the vaginal opening. This is the entrance to the inner sex organs, through which menstrual flow leaves the body. The male inserts his penis here during sexual intercourse, and this is the end of the passage through which a baby is born. Beginning during puberty, a girl may notice that her vaginal opening feels wet. This is due to secretions triggered by hormonal changes.

In many, but by no means all, young girls, the vaginal opening is covered by a thin piece of membrane called the hymen. The hymen usually has one or several holes in it so the menstrual flow can escape. Sometimes the hymen is simply a fringe of tissue around the perimeter of the vaginal opening. Many cultures believe it important that when a girl "loses her virginity" (has intercourse for the first time) the hymen is "broken" with some pain and bleeding. Not too much emphasis should be placed on this, because the hymen varies so much from girl to girl that many girls do not experience this.

The outer and inner lips join together beneath the vaginal opening. Across a narrow band of skin is the final opening—the anus, from which fecal matter exits the body.

The Vagina

The vaginal opening leads to the vagina, which joins the external sex organs to the internal reproductive system. It is a short, narrow passage with a tremendous capacity to stretch and shrink back to normal. It is narrow enough to hold a tampon in place, yet it can stretch to allow the birth of a baby.

Young girls, on hearing the facts of life, might panic, not understanding how the narrow vagina can accommodate a man's penis during sex. They need to be reassured that in the first stages of sexual excitement the vagina expands enough to accept a penis of any size, and also that the smooth walls of the vagina lubricate during arousal to make penetration easy.

Internal Organs

At the top of the vagina is a tiny opening called the cervix. It leads into the uterus—a hollow, pouchlike organ where the baby grows when a woman becomes pregnant. In an adult woman the uterus, shaped generally like a downward-pointing triangle, is about the same size as her clenched fist. Like the vagina, it too is very elastic and its muscular walls can expand to accommodate a growing fetus.

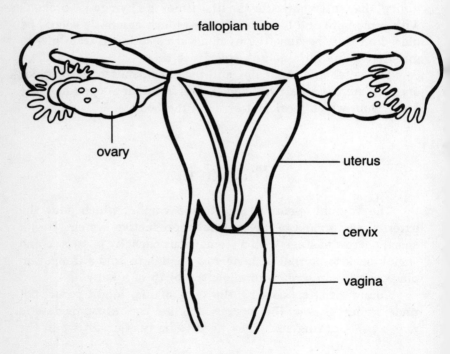

fallopian tube

ovary

uterus

cervix

vagina

Leading into both upper corners of the uterus are narrow tubes called the fallopian tubes. The two fallopian tubes connect to the ovaries, small, walnut-sized organs that house the ova (eggs). Girls are born with all the ova that they will ever have—usually about two million, most of which die during childhood. By puberty, when the ova become mature, about a half million are left. How these ripen, one by one, during the menstrual cycle is explained in the next chapter.

CHAPTER SIX

Menstruation

The best time to talk to a girl about her periods is before she gets the first one. Even though she might have heard about menstruation from friends, she might not quite believe it without confirmation from a trusted adult. The sight of blood on her clothing can be quite frightening, even traumatic, if she is not prepared. Also, if you have never broken the ice about menstruation with her, it might be difficult and embarrassing for her to come to you now that she has begun to have periods.

A few months before she starts menstruating, a girl will usually have some white or yellowish vaginal discharge that you will see in her underwear. This, along with the previously mentioned outward signs of puberty, should tip you off that her first period is impending. So if the subject has not come up before, now would be a good time to have that talk.

Every home has its own way of handling such matters. Some families are very open and communicative, with every member participating in the lives of all the others. There are families where an event such as a girl's first menstrual period is talked about around the dinner table, and even celebrated.

In other instances, you will have to overcome your own shyness or discomfort with the topic, to avoid transmitting such attitudes to your daughter. If you have difficulty talking about menstruation, begin your discussions with a simplified version of the facts.

All healthy women on earth between menarche (the start of menstruation) and menopause ("the change of life")—roughly half the population of the world—menstruate. Menstruation is one of the few physical constants in the adult woman's life. You would imagine that these facts alone would be enough to divest the subject of the shroud of mystery and myth it is under!

But somehow what is actually a sign of good health and fertility is too often regarded as something sick or dirty. There were times when a menstruating woman was thought to curdle milk, blight crops, wilt flowers, spoil food, cause death, and be responsible for storms!

In more recent times women who had their periods refrained from swimming or washing their hair, drinking cold drinks, or exercising for fear of causing cramps or prolonging the flow. We now know, of course, that none of this has any validity. Better education and the proliferation of books, magazines, television, and radio talk shows that readily discuss such personal matters have exposed most of us to the realities of menstruation.

But even the most sophisticated women sometimes have difficulty in talking to their daughters about this natural phenomenon in terms other than "the curse," "the monthlies," "a visit from a friend," "on the rag," or "that time of month." One of the best ways you can instill in your daughter a healthy attitude about the subject is by not using these archaic and misleading terms.

The most commonly accepted description is "menstrual period," or "period" for short. The word "menstrual" derives from the Latin *mens* meaning "month," which makes sense since a menstrual cycle takes roughly a month to complete. But *mens,* in turn, is derived from the word for moon, and it's thought that the ancient Romans believed the menstrual period was somehow cosmically controlled by the waxing and waning of the moon.

Modern medical science has taught us that the menstrual cycle is controlled by a complicated interaction of nervous signals and hormonal responses that ready the woman's body for pregnancy on a regular basis. In order for a girl to know exactly what a period is and why she gets it, it helps to understand the reproductive cycle.

The Menstrual Cycle

The menstrual cycle consists of all the days from one period to the next. It starts with the first day of menstruation and ends the day before the following period starts. The average cycle is twenty-eight days long, but it is perfectly normal to have a cycle

of twenty-one to thirty-five days. Some women are very regular. They have cycles of the same length every month. Others find that their cycle varies from month to month. Some women have one cycle for years, then inexplicably change to another.

Equally variable is the length and intensity of individual women's periods. It's not unusual for some women to menstruate for only two days and others for six days. The average is five days. Some women have the heaviest flow at the beginning of their period; for others it's the reverse.

When a young girl first starts getting her periods, she is often quite irregular. She can go months between periods, and sometimes they will be heavy, other times light. It usually takes a year or two for her to settle down into her own menstrual rhythm.

It's important that your daughter understand this, because she may become alarmed and think something is wrong with her if she misses a period. The reason her periods are not regular at first is because she has not started ovulating regularly.

About once a month, the brain releases a substance called follicle stimulating hormone (FSH) that starts to ripen one of the ova. Usually it ripens eggs from alternating ovaries—the right one month, the left the following month. It takes about ten to twelve days for the egg to ripen. When the ovum is ripe, it sets off down the fallopian tube on its journey to the uterus. That journey takes from one to three days to complete. If, during those days, a woman has sexual intercourse, the ovum can be fertilized by the male's sperm and the woman becomes pregnant. This happens in the middle of the cycle, about fifteen days before the cycle's end.

Many girls are confused about when during the menstrual cycle they can become pregnant. It is important that you make sure that she knows that her most fertile time is when she is ovulating.

Some women can tell when they are ovulating because they get a slight pain or achy feeling in their lower abdomen for a day—sort of "minicramps." This is known as mittelschmerz, a German expression for "pain in the middle."

While this is going on, the hormones estrogen and progesterone stimulate the growth of a spongy, nutritious, blood-rich lining (the endometrium) in the uterus. This will feed and protect the fetus should the woman become pregnant. If the ovum reaches the uterus without being fertilized, this lining is not needed.

Consequently, at the end of the cycle, the uterus sloughs off the endometrium, which exits the body as menstrual flow. This flow, usually referred to as blood, is actually a mixture of tissue, mucus, and some blood. The color of the flow can vary from a dark rusty brown to bright blood-red, and it can have clots or lumps. It leaves the uterus by way of the cervix, the narrow opening between the uterus and the vagina, then flows down the vagina, and out through the vaginal opening. The day after the flow starts—day one of the new cycle—the brain triggers off the whole process again.

An additional aspect of the cycle is the mucosal discharge from the vagina. This discharge varies in amount and consistency during the cycle and from woman to woman. Women who have a mucosal discharge often find that right after their periods they are quite dry. Closer to ovulation they produce some opaque mucus. At ovulation one of two things can happen: they either feel very wet for a few days, or they get blobs of a gummy discharge that looks a bit like egg whites. This is known as spinnbarkeit (spinn, for short) mucus, and many women cite its presence as an indication that they are at their most fertile. When the spinn disappears, it may be replaced by an opaque white or yellowish discharge which becomes clear and watery a day or two before the onset of the next period.

These changes are brought about by hormonal fluctuations. A girl should become familiar with them, because any unusual change in volume or odor can indicate that she has an infection that needs attention from a doctor.

This monthly cycle of events, once started at puberty, continues until a woman reaches the end of her fertile years, usually in her late forties or early fifties.

Protection

Of course, as soon as your daughter starts menstruating, you will have to provide her with something to use to absorb the flow. Interestingly (and with good judgment!), napkin and tampon manufacturers have tended to stop using the word "sanitary" when referring to their products. Use of this word in the past has only furthered the notion that periods are something "unsanitary," and you would do well to follow their lead.

For many adult women, getting a box of napkins from their mothers was the only exchange they had with them about menstruation.

> "I got my first period when I was eleven. I didn't know what to do, and I just hid my stained underpants in the back of a drawer. Obviously, my mother found them because the next day they were gone and there was a box of napkins and a belt in the drawer. Nobody ever told me how to use them, I had to figure it out for myself. The worst thing was that I didn't know how to get rid of the used pads. I was always trying to flush them down the toilet and getting it blocked."
>
> Sandy, age eighteen

You can help your daughter avoid a great deal of anxiety by teaching her not only about what is available in the way of protection, but how to buy it, use it, and dispose of it. Don't assume that these things are obvious, and remember that your daughter is dealing with the situation for the first time.

In fact, you might consider buying your daughter a "starter kit" of supplies months before she needs them. That way she can become familiar with how various products look, feel, and work and won't be intimidated. Also, she will have materials on hand when she gets her first period, and will be spared the possible embarrassment of having to ask for supplies.

Napkins

There is a huge variety of napkins available today. By and large the uncomfortable belts of recent years have been replaced by adhesive strips that stick to your underpants. Napkins come in several thicknesses, shapes, and sizes. Some are designed specifically for young girls, scaled down to fit smaller women. Don't automatically assume that the product you use is best for your daughter.

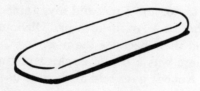

Buy several different kinds for her to try. Let her decide what is most comfortable and offers the best protection. Chances are she will discuss the matter with her friends and might have some ideas about what she would like to try.

Another good idea is to take her with you when you buy napkins. At some time she will have to buy her own, and this can be a source of embarrassment to young girls. If she goes shopping with you and sees you put a box in your grocery cart or

shopping basket, she will soon realize that nobody stared or even noticed the purchase. Make sure she knows what kind of stores carry napkins (grocery, convenience, drug, supermarket) and how much they cost.

Explain that many public restrooms have machines where she can buy napkins or tampons in an emergency. You might consider calling her school and asking the office where or from whom your daughter can get a pad if she unexpectedly gets her period there.

Also, help her get into the habit of carrying a pad or tampon in her bag so she will have something on hand when she needs it. Until she becomes regular, her periods will be unpredictable, and knowing that she has protection nearby might help her feel more secure.

Many girls worry about staying clean while menstruating.

Napkins should be replaced every four to six hours, more often if the flow is heavy. Menstrual flow is sterile, but as with sweat, when it comes into contact with the bacteria on your body or in the air, it can start to smell bad. Changing napkins regularly, wearing clean underwear, and bathing daily can ensure this does not happen. It is unwise to use perfumed or deodorant napkins as these only bring chemicals in contact with delicate skin.

Girls who have a fair amount of vaginal discharge between periods might feel comfortable using a thin pad or "panty liner" at those times.

Finally, make sure your daughter knows how to dispose of a soiled napkin. Pads should not be flushed as they can block the plumbing. Furthermore, many pads now contain a lot of plastic, which is not biodegradable. Some brands come individually wrapped in a little pouch which can be used to rewrap the pad for disposal. Pads can also be put into plastic sandwich bags or wrapped in paper and then placed in the garbage or incinerator. If there are several women in your household, put a small flip-top canister lined with plastic in your bathroom into which soiled pads can be placed. The canister should be emptied and relined daily.

Tampons

There is no physical reason why a young or virginal girl cannot use tampons, though some feel uncomfortable doing so because they are invasive in nature. A tampon will not injure the hymen. With gentle application and perhaps the use of a lubricant such as K-Y jelly, anyone should be able to insert at least a junior-size or slender tampon.

Offer your daughter tampons as an option because there is no doubt that they are more comfortable, convenient, and liberating than napkins for most women. They are easier to carry

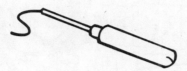

around, and to dispose of (simply flush). Again, let your daughter try different kinds: those with applicators and those without. She probably will want to experiment with them in private, but first take one from the package and show her what it looks like. Make sure she has the instruction leaflet to follow as various brands require different methods of insertion.

Young girls often express concerns about tampons getting lost inside them. Assure her that there is nowhere for it to go. The cervix is the only other opening in the vagina, and it is much too narrow to let a tampon through: it would be like trying to pass an orange through a buttonhole. The worst that can happen is that the string will recoil into the vagina, making the tampon difficult to remove. Even then, the string can easily be found with the fingers and pulled back out.

A tampon should never be left in place for more than six hours. After that it can start to harbor bacteria. If the flow is heavy, tampons should be changed more often, but not too frequently, as this can lead to abrasions or irritation of the vagina. For the same reason, a tampon should never be used between periods.

Toxic-Shock Syndrome (TSS)

TSS is a rare, occasionally fatal disease. When it first came to national prominence in the early 1980s, a large percentage of the cases reported were in menstruating women using tampons. Women under thirty and teenage girls seemed to be particularly vulnerable. The medical profession concluded that overly absorbent tampons created conditions that were conducive to the growth of *Staphylococcus aureus,* the bacteria causing the disease. Furthermore, these tampons caused scratches and sores on the wall of the vagina which further fostered the growth of bacteria.

In the ensuing years, incidences of this disease have diminished as manufacturers have changed the composition of tampons, women have started using them differently, and familiarity with the symptoms of TSS has led women to seek medical help sooner.

It's a good idea to get a girl into the habit of using tampons safely from the outset. She should:

- use tampons only during the day, pads at night

- use the minimum-absorbency tampon necessary—there's no need to use a "super" on light days

- know the symptoms of TSS, which are a sudden high fever of at least 102 degrees; vomiting and watery diarrhea; a sunburnlike rash, mainly on the hands and feet; fainting and dizziness caused by a drop in blood pressure; and possibly flulike symptoms of headache, sore throat, and muscle pain.

Dysmenorrhea

Dysmenorrhea is the clinical name for menstrual cramps or period pain. In 1957 a group of English doctors isolated hormonelike substances called prostaglandins in menstruating women, and several years later these chemicals were discovered to be directly responsible for cramping. Women who suffer the most severe pain are found to have higher levels of the substances.

Prior to this discovery, many doctors subscribed to the "it's all in your head" school of gynecology. While suffering women knew only too well that it wasn't all in their heads, they did not think there was anything they could do about the pain.

"The only thing my mom told me about periods was that she had suffered through them for twenty years and that I would have to do the same. It wasn't until I went away to college that I found out that I could actually get some help from the doctor. At first I was furious with my mom—then I felt sorry for her because she just didn't know any better."

Belinda, age nineteen

The point is, this generation is the first to benefit from these medical breakthroughs, so it's up to you to break the chain of misinformation. No girl or woman should suffer unnecessarily from incapacitating dysmenorrhea.

A girl prone to cramps will usually start experiencing them once she has started ovulating and menstruating regularly. This condition is known as primary dysmenorrhea, as opposed to sec-

ondary dysmenorrhea, which affects older women. In primary dysmenorrhea the prostaglandins stimulate the muscles of the uterus to spasm, leading to cramping pain in the pelvic area. At best this can cause mild discomfort; at its worst the pain can be devastating, extending to the legs and back, and accompanied by fainting, vomiting, and diarrhea. The symptoms can last anywhere from twenty-four hours to three days.

In mild cases a woman can often gain relief by holding a hot-water bottle or heating pad against her abdomen, taking a soak in a hot tub, or having a hot drink. As with all physical matters, a healthy lifestyle incorporating regular exercise and good nutrition also helps.

Severe pain can be eased by the use of antiprostaglandin drugs such as aspirin or ibuprofen, which are available over the counter (without a prescription). If your daughter goes to school carrying these drugs, be sure she has a note from you identifying the medications and stating that she has your permission to use them. Better yet, get a note from a doctor. You would do well to have a doctor's approval for the use of these drugs, especially in very young girls. (Aspirin has been found to trigger a disease called Reye's syndrome in some children.) In any event, severe pain is a good reason for the girl to have a physical checkup.

Despite modern drugs and progressive attitudes, some women just feel so ill at this time of month that they have no choice but to take off a day or two from their regular routine and rest. There is no reason to feel apologetic about this—the pain is real. Try to help your daughter strike a balance between not letting her periods disrupt her life unnecessarily and being too stalwart about the discomfort she feels.

CHAPTER SEVEN

Hygiene and Health

As has been previously mentioned, the vagina is naturally very clean, in fact cleaner than the mouth. However, a problem can arise if a harmful organism, one that upsets the natural balance of benign bacteria, is introduced to the area. The vagina is warm, moist, and dark—ideal conditions for the proliferation of harmful bacteria.

Irritation or burning in the genital area, without any accompanying discharge, can be caused by something as simple as too-tight clothing, excessive sweating during summer or while exercising, or a sensitivity to soap or lotions. The symptoms can usually be brought under control by changing the conditions causing them, washing frequently with cool water, and using a mild medicated cream to break the itch-scratch-itch cycle. If itching persists, the young woman should see a doctor to make sure that she does not have an infection of some kind.

If the itching is accompanied by an unusually heavy or discolored discharge, the woman may have a form of vaginitis. Vaginitis is a catchall name for infections of the genital area. They can be caused by any number of factors including diet, medication, general health conditions, cuts and scratches, and allergies. This distinguishes them from sexually transmitted diseases (STDs), which can be transmitted *only* by sexual contact.

This distinction is very important. The media is so full of frightening reports and statistics about STDs that a girl might be frightened, thinking that she has contracted something far more serious than a mild infection. Let her know that she can come to you if she notices any sign that something is not quite right. Symptoms in a girl who is not sexually active probably indicate one of the following:

• Moniliasis or candidiasis, commonly referred to as a yeast infection. Its symptoms are severe itching, a red and swollen vulva, and a thick, white, cottage-cheeselike discharge with a faint yeasty smell. Occasionally there will also be a burning sensation when urinating.

• Trichomoniasis, often called "trich," also causes itching and burning. Its discharge is thin, foamy, yellowish, and quite foul-smelling. The odor is sometimes the first noticeable symptom.

• Nonspecific vaginitis, which produces a grayish and particularly bad-smelling discharge. Usually, though, there is little itching.

If your daughter has any of these symptoms, don't try to cure them yourself. Take her to a doctor, who will prescribe drugs or suppositories that will take care of the problem, usually within a couple of weeks.

Sexually Transmitted Diseases

Aside from AIDS, which is discussed later in this chapter, there is something of an epidemic of sexually transmitted diseases (STDs) in this country. The American Social Health Association reports that one in four Americans between the ages of fifteen and fifty-five will get an STD during their lifetime. More than ten million people a year see a doctor because of these problems.

Women are particularly vulnerable when it comes to STDs. They are more likely than men to contract these diseases from a single exposure. Often a woman doesn't know she's caught anything because the symptoms are not always immediately apparent. Consequently she can suffer serious complications from an STD because the disease goes undetected until it has reached a dangerous stage. Additionally, if a woman has an STD when she is pregnant, the disease can cause miscarriage, premature birth, infant death, and blindness or other birth defects.

As you can see, it is of vital importance that from a young age women are aware of the dangers of, and learn how to prevent, recognize, and remedy STDs.

The most obvious way to not get an STD, of course, is to not have sex. But, assuming that we are talking about people who are sexually active, there are two points that should be stressed in terms of prevention. A girl must know with whom she is sleeping. It's not usually possible to learn someone's complete sexual history overnight, and even if she asks he might lie. But at the very least, before having sex, a woman should know a man well enough to get an idea of his sexual habits: how promiscuous he is or has been, whether he is in the habit of using a condom during sex, whether he has ever had and can recognize an STD. This is not so that she can make value judgments about his lifestyle, but to protect her life. Indiscriminate, casual sex is tantamount to Russian roulette.

The second way to help prevent STDs is to stress the importance of insisting that any new lover use a condom until the woman knows him well enough to be certain that he is not infected. Condoms and, to a lesser extent, other barrier contraceptives like the diaphragm (and spermicides) are fairly, though not totally, effective for this purpose. These days many women are buying condoms rather than relying on a man to supply

them. If your daughter is sexually active, or is planning to be, you could do worse than to ensure that she is familiar with condoms, knows where to buy them, and how they are used.

More than twenty communicable diseases can be contracted from having sex. The following are some of the most rampant.

• Gonorrhea. Colloquially known as "the clap," gonorrhea is contracted by more than two million Americans a year. Gonorrhea primarily infects sex organs, but can also infect the throat and eyes. The symptoms are vaginal discharge, slight burning on urination, and sometimes lower abdominal pain and fever. But here's the frightening part: there is an eighty percent chance that a woman won't have any symptoms. Men display symptoms far more often than do women. It's important that you make it clear to your daughter that if someone she sleeps with is infected, but she doesn't appear to be, she should still be tested for the disease.

In any case, women should have a gonorrhea culture taken when they have their annual gynecological checkup, and immediately on becoming pregnant. Should the test prove positive, the disease can be treated with a shot of penicillin or other antibiotics. One strain of gonorrhea is resistant to penicillin—a variety contracted by soldiers in Vietnam. But drugs have been found to treat it, and it has not become the out-of-hand menace that people once feared.

If caught early, gonorrhea can be cured with no lasting side effects, but if it's left untreated the results can be extremely serious. Unchecked gonorrhea can lead to pelvic inflammatory disease (PID), and at its worst, PID can cause scarring in the fallopian tubes, ectopic (tubal) pregnancies, and infertility.

• Chlamydia. This may be an unfamiliar name to you, but it is the leading STD in the United States. About five million people a year contract this parasite, which establishes itself in the cervix or in the urethra.

Once again, this disease often has no symptoms. If they do manifest, the symptoms can be mistaken for gonorrhea. Once diagnosed, chlamydia can be treated with tetracycline. Like gonorrhea, chlamydia can cause PID and problem pregnancies. More than ten thousand women a year become sterile as a result of chlamydia-induced PID.

• Pubic Lice. Commonly called "crabs," pubic lice are minute bugs that infest pubic hair and cause intense itching. The lice lay their eggs at the base of the hairs and, in about ten days to two weeks, the larvae develop into adults that, under a microscope, look like the crabs seen at the beach.

Apart from the itching, a girl with crabs might notice pinpoints of blood on her underwear or pubic area. On close examination she will see the tiny creatures moving among her pubic hairs.

Lice can be eradicated with a prescription shampoo called Kwell, or a pharmacist can recommend an over-the-counter medicine. Sheets, towels, washcloths, and underwear will have to be washed thoroughly in boiling water. There is a potential for reinfection since the parasites can live for a short time apart from their human hosts. Unlike all other STDs, which *cannot* be contracted from public places, there is a chance that crabs can be caught by sharing a towel, sleeping over at someone's house, or wearing someone else's clothing.

There are no known serious or lasting effects

from lice. The problems they cause are mainly social and embarrassing.

• Genital Warts. Although you don't hear as much about them, genital warts are more common than herpes. They are quite different from the warts that children often get on their hands or feet. Genital warts are caused by a virus and are highly contagious. Not only can they be passed to and from sexual partners, but they also spread rapidly on your own body. They appear about a month after contact, and are usually small, flesh-colored or whitish growths.

It is tempting to ignore these warts because they are not painful. But your daughter should pay attention to them because the Centers for Disease Control believe that there is a link between genital warts and cancer of the cervix, vagina, and anus. Furthermore, many doctors insist on a caesarean birth if the mother has this condition, because the baby can be infected.

Warts can be removed by burning, freezing, surgery, or drying out with chemicals. These remedies are not particularly pleasant, so it is worth getting warts treated as soon as they appear and before they spread.

• Herpes. Herpes is a virus of which there are two strains. HSV-1 is the one that causes cold sores on the face; HSV-2 is known as genital herpes. About 500,000 people a year get herpes—and right now there is no cure.

At one time it was thought that the two types of virus could infect only those parts of the body on which they originated. But this is not the case. HSV-1 can be transmitted to the genital area, and

HSV-2 to the face, through touch. Instruct your daughter that she must practice scrupulous hygiene if she gets a cold sore on her face. She should touch the lesion as little as possible, and wash her hands well before using the toilet or changing tampons or pads.

The first sign of herpes is a small, itchy, red bump. This quickly turns into a cluster of painful blisters. This stage is highly infectious, and the sufferer should avoid all sex. The first outbreak may be accompanied by a low fever, muscle aches, and a general feeling of being under the weather. (Some people never have a second outbreak, others have occasional outbreaks, and some unlucky sufferers get one attack after another.)

Within two weeks the sores will heal but the virus, unfortunately, does not go away. It retreats into the body, waiting for something to weaken the body's immune system. That something can be stress (exams, vacations, family holidays, moving to a new school or town, travel), bad nutrition, tiredness, or another illness. If any of these things occur just before a girl gets her period, her chances of an outbreak are increased. Studies have shown a possible link between herpes outbreaks and an increase in prostaglandins—the substances that also cause cramps.

Some medical professionals feel that the dangers of herpes have been grossly exaggerated by the media, and that those who have it have been made to feel unduly "unclean." In fact, herpes in itself is a mild illness. But it has been linked to cervical cancer: women with genital herpes have a much greater chance of getting this disease. It is very important, therefore, that women with herpes not neglect their annual Pap test.

The other serious consequence of herpes is its danger to newborns. The disease does not touch the baby while it is in the womb, but if the mother is having an attack when she delivers, the baby might be fatally affected.

Though there is no cure yet for herpes, a few years ago the Food and Drug Administration approved a substance called acyclovir as a herpes medication. In some people it helps shorten the duration and severity of the symptoms.

- AIDS (Acquired Immune Deficiency Syndrome). AIDS has become the scourge of the twentieth century. So much has been written, broadcast, and said about this incurable and fatal disease that there is a danger of young people becoming blasé about it. Furthermore, teenagers tend to have feelings of immortality and assume that "it can't happen to me." But it can, and it is imperative that you make sure that your children are educated on the subject. Information is easy to come by. Most urban centers run AIDS hotlines, your local hospital or doctor will have pamphlets, and gay organizations are usually ahead of the mainstream in keeping up with and disseminating AIDS information.

As far as researchers presently know, the AIDS virus (actually, the HIV virus) is transmitted only through the transfer of bodily fluids, namely blood and semen. AIDS cannot be caught by casual contact, which includes kissing, hugging, holding hands, sharing drinking glasses, and so forth. A woman can get it by having vaginal, anal, or oral intercourse with an infected man—if his contaminated sperm enters her bloodstream through minute tears in her tissue, or if she swallows his sperm. She can also contract the disease if she's given a transfusion of blood from an HIV carrier. This is increasingly unlikely, since all blood is now stringently tested. The virus is also transmitted through sharing hypodermic needles with a carrier.

Most women who have contracted the disease are either intravenous drug users or have had sex with men who are either intravenous drug users or bisexual. Because the virus can lie dormant and a carrier can display no symptoms, the Centers for Disease Control advise women to take precautions with men who have had even one homosexual experience in the last ten years. AIDS educators point out that when you have sex with someone, you are sexually linked with all the other people he or she has slept with, plus all the people those people have slept with—a permutation that can add up to hundreds of thousands of possible HIV carriers. Anyone who thinks they might possibly have been exposed to HIV should be tested, not only for their own peace of mind, but to ensure they do not pass on the disease.

Early symptoms of AIDS are persistently swollen glands in the neck, armpit, or groin, an inexplicable and rapid weight loss, tiredness, white spots in the mouth, and a long-lasting sore throat and dry cough.

The Gynecologist

Once your daughter's periods have become regular, start thinking about her first gynecological checkup, especially if she has been experiencing menstrual pain or heavy or unusual bleeding, or if she has any of the symptoms described above. Even if everything is just fine, the soaring rate of teenage pregnancies reveals that today's young girls are making decisions about sex very soon after starting their periods. So, while it might be hard for you to deal with, it's wise to introduce your daughter to a sympathetic professional who can give her the advice she will need if and when she opts to use birth control.

How to choose a gynecologist? Let your daughter be part of the process. If you are happy with your own, suggest him or her, but also offer an alternative. "Would you like to see Dr. Benbow? I've been very happy with him for five years. Or would you like us to try to find a doctor who specializes in treating younger patients?" Don't be surprised if your daughter declines to see your own doctor. Many girls feel uncomfortable going to their mother's doctor because they are (usually unjustifiably) afraid he or she will break a confidence. It could be something more straightforward, such as your doctor being a man and your daughter feeling more comfortable with a woman. Abide by her wishes if she asks to find her own doctor.

Many gynecologists specialize in treating adolescents. Your pediatrician might be able to recommend one, or you or your daughter can ask friends for a name or call a referral service connected with a reputable hospital.

The first examination can be fraught with anxiety for a young girl if she doesn't know what to expect. Explain what is going to happen to her.

Most exams roughly follow this procedure:

> • The doctor or a nurse will take a medical history. This can include some potentially embarrassing questions including whether or not the girl has had sexual intercourse. Stress to your daughter that it is in her own interest to answer the questions honestly, and that the doctor is bound by a code of ethics not to discuss this information with anyone—including you!

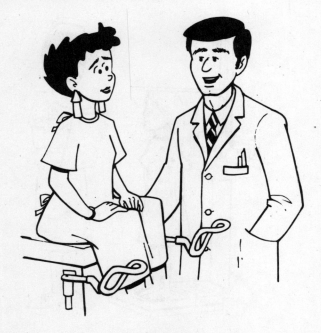

• The girl will then take off her clothes and put on a gown. She will never be totally nude at any time during the examination. A nurse will weigh and measure her and take her blood pressure, pulse, and temperature. The girl may also be asked to provide urine for testing, and to evacuate her bladder to make the internal exam easier.

• The doctor will feel the glands in the woman's neck, throat and armpits, then do a breast exam similar to the self-exam described earlier. Then he or she will probably palpate the patient's abdomen.

• Next comes the internal examination. The girl will lie on the table with her knees bent and separated—possibly with her feet in stirrups. The doctor will look at the outside of the genital area. Then, if the girl is very young or has a thick hymen, the doctor will examine her internally with a gloved finger and a swab. Usually, however, he or she will insert a speculum—a metal or plastic device that allows him or her to look inside the vagina and see the cervix.

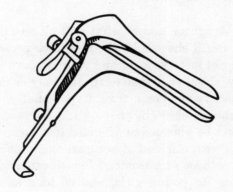

Once a year, or on some other regular basis, the doctor will take a Pap smear. To do this, he or she inserts a cotton swab into the vagina and rotates the end of the swab against the cervix. A few cells from the cervix will stick to the swab and are transferred to a glass plate that will be sent to a laboratory for analysis. This reveals any irregularities in the early stages.

The patient should feel free to ask questions about what the doctor is doing at any point.

Your own attitude in explaining this procedure is vital in shaping your daughter's feelings toward this important part of her health regimen. So don't describe the exam as embarrassing, scary, painful (which it shouldn't be), or something to be dreaded. Keep your language matter-of-fact, and stress the benefits, which are:

- Early detection of any infections or diseases

- Confirmation of pregnancy

- Ensuring the general health and well-being of a woman's reproductive system

- Prescription of an appropriate and effective method of birth control

Once your daughter knows what will go on during the examination, ask her if she would like you to be present. Depending on a number of factors, including your rapport with her, her sense of privacy, shyness, and so forth, she may or may not want you there. Either way, don't take it personally, and having given her the choice, abide by it.

Finally, don't be alarmed or offended if it turns out that she would rather go with a friend of her own age or to a clinic such as Planned Parenthood or a women's health center. This is often less intimidating for young girls, and as long as the clinic is reputable, it is a viable option.

CHAPTER EIGHT

Boys and Sex

Just as they are curious about their own bodies, pubescent girls will have lots of questions about male anatomy. Be prepared to answer them in a straightforward manner. This is also a good lead-in to an explanation of sexual intercourse.

During puberty, boys undergo many changes similar to those that girls experience. They get taller and heavier and their muscle strength increases, their skin gets oilier, they begin to sweat more, and they grow body hair. Additionally, boys' voices "break," becoming deeper, they grow facial hair, their penises and testicles get bigger, and they begin to manufacture sperm and semen.

Many girls will have seen their brothers undressed or pictures or statues of naked men, and know that males have testicles and penises. But knowing this probably raises more questions than it answers.

The penis is the organ that hangs between a male's legs. In its normal, flaccid state it can vary in size and length, and it has a tube, the urethra, running through it. Boys both urinate and ejaculate through this tube. When a boy becomes sexually aroused, nerve centers at the base of his spinal cord send messages to the brain which cause blood to rush into the blood vessels and spongy tissue in the penis. This causes the penis to become longer, wider, harder, and darker in color, and to stand erect. Regardless of its size when flaccid, a full-grown man's penis, when erect, is usually five to six inches long. An erect

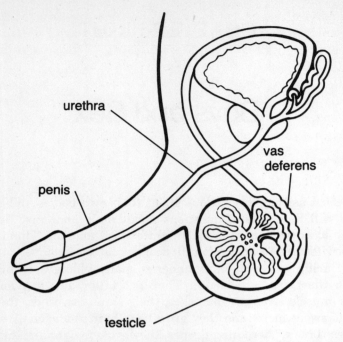

urethra

vas
deferens

penis

testicle

penis can be so rigid that it is often referred to as a "hard-on" or
a "boner."

Muscles at the base of the penis tighten so that the blood
can't drain back out while a male has an erection, and a valve
shuts off the entry from the bladder so no urine can come out. In
other words, a boy cannot pee while he has an erection.

Sperm—the male counterpart to the female's ova—are
made in tubes which are tightly coiled inside the testicles, the
two egg-shaped organs that hang below and behind the penis
and which are commonly referred to as "balls." Just as with
girls, boys' anatomies can vary from person to person. It is quite
normal for a boy to have one testicle bigger or longer than the
other.

Millions of sperm are manufactured each day. When they
are mature, they move through tubes called the vas deferens
(which are what are cut and tied during a vasectomy) to com-

partments inside the boy's body called seminal vesicles, where they are stored until the male ejaculates or "comes." Ejaculate is a creamy liquid that consists of sperm and a fluid called semen that is made in the seminal vesicle.

Boys ejaculate during orgasms reached by masturbation, having sexual intercourse, or simply becoming aroused by thinking or dreaming about sexy things. When a boy ejaculates during his sleep it is called a "wet dream."

> "I had this really sexy dream that seemed to go on all night. When I started to wake up it felt so real that I couldn't figure out what was going on. Then when I woke up properly I realized that my pajamas were all wet. I was kind of surprised, but I knew what had happened and I was also kind of happy."
>
> Eric, age thirteen

This usually begins to happen between the ages of eleven and fifteen. For boys, beginning to ejaculate is a bit like girls beginning to menstruate—it's a sign that they are becoming adults. And both of these events signify that the girl or boy is old enough to create a pregnancy.

There are about *400 million* sperm in an ejaculation, and it only takes *one* to fertilize a ripe ovum. There are also sperm in the drops of fluid that ooze from a boy's penis when it is erect but before he has an orgasm. One tiny drop of ejaculate deposited in the vagina, or even near the vaginal opening, is all it takes. It is very important that your children know this, and that if they are going to have sex, they must use some method of birth control. Despite these seemingly sophisticated times, young people still fall prey to myths about pregnancy: you can't get pregnant the first time you have sex, or if you do it standing up, or if the boy pulls out before he comes, or if you douche right after. None of these, of course, are true. And all of them have led to the heartbreak of teenage pregnancies.

Fortunately, the incidence of teenage pregnancy has declined a little over the last few years. But that doesn't mean teenagers are having sex less often. Teen sex is epidemic, and the drop in the pregnancy rate is believed to be due to education about and availability of contraceptives.

Whatever morals, ethics, or philosophies about sex you impart to your children, you cannot dictate their behavior. If they choose to have sex, they should be knowledgeable about what contraceptive options are open to them.

> • **The Pill.** This is a daily dose of hormones that tricks the woman's body into not ripening an ovum every month. There is, therefore, nothing for the male sperm to fertilize. It's almost thirty years since the Pill revolutionized women's lives. Many of the serious side effects that got so much press in the early days have been largely eliminated in recent years by the introduction of minipills. These have only one hormone, progestin—a synthetic version of progesterone—rather than a combination of estrogen and progestin.
>
> The Pill often causes minor side effects such as nausea, headaches, weight gain, enlarged breasts, and patches of discolored skin, but these usually vanish after a couple of months. Also, these negatives are to some extent balanced by the Pill's

positive effects: regular periods, and the alleviation of cramps

The Pill is an ideal method of birth control for a healthy, sexually active teenager or young woman. If used correctly it is almost foolproof, certainly convenient, and definitely the least embarrassing method to use—a big plus for a young woman. As it can only be prescribed by a doctor, it also tends to ensure that a girl gets regular check-ups.

• **The IUD.** A once-popular method of contraception is the IUD or intrauterine device. This was placed inside the woman's uterus by her physician and prevented conception or implantation of a fertilized egg. But many women suffered severe, sometimes fatal, side effects, and many types of IUDs were discontinued. They are almost never used today in the United States.

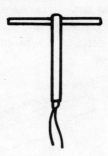

• **Barrier Methods.** These operate by blocking the passage of sperm to the uterus. This can be done mechanically, with a diaphragm, a cervical cap, a sponge, or a condom; or chemically with a spermicide. Usually, it's a combination of both. Condoms are highly touted by the medical profession because they offer sexually active people the only available, if incomplete, protection against STDs.

—The diaphragm. This is a round, dome-shaped rubber device with a spring in its rim it fits over the cervix. It works in conjunction with a spermicidal cream or jelly that is squeezed into the dome before insertion. It should be put in place not more than two hours before having sex, and left in for at least six hours afterward. Diaphragms come in different sizes and have to be fitted by a doctor or nurse practitioner who will also teach the art of diaphragm insertion. It can be tricky at first, but as with tampons, after a little practice in private it will become easy. The diaphragm can be ideal for a girl who is at ease touching her own body and is self-possessed enough to handle contraception at the time of having sex. It takes a certain measure of maturity to effectively use a diaphragm. It's less than ideal for teenagers who are irresponsible, squeamish, or shy.

—The cervical cap. A small version of the diaphragm, the cervical cap fits over the cervix but is kept in place by suction rather than spring tension. It was available in Europe for many years before only recently becoming available in the United States. It can be left in place for several days and so doesn't interfere with spontaneity, but many girls find the cap difficult to insert and remove. As with the diaphragm, it has to be fitted by a doctor or at a clinic.

—**The sponge.** This is the newest barrier contraceptive on the market. The sponge has triple action: it blocks the cervix, releases a spermicide, and absorbs the sperm. It's relatively easy to insert as it is soft and has no springs or suction. Once in place it is effective for twenty-four hours. The other big advantage is that it does not need to be fitted by a doctor and is available from a pharmacy or market. As it is such a self-contained unit and has a long shelf life, it could be the ideal contraceptive to keep in a purse.

—**The condom.** Condoms are the oldest reliable method of contraception, but were neglected as an option for many years. Now, because of the AIDS scare, they are back in popularity with a vengeance. Also known as "rubbers," condoms offer protection from STDs, are an efficient method of birth control (especially when used with a spermicide), are cheap, easily obtainable, convenient, and free from side effects. Once regarded as a "man's" contraceptive, condoms are now being bought by women for their own protection. Most condoms are penis-length sheaths of thin latex that come rolled up in packets. Condoms made of "skin" or other natural materials are available, but they are not as effective as latex in preventing the transmission of HIV or other sexually transmitted diseases. Some brands are lubricated or contain built-in spermicides. The male unrolls one onto his erect penis before he inserts it into the female's vagina. After he ejaculates, he should hold on to the base of the condom and withdraw right away. If he waits until his penis has become flaccid, the condom might come off and the semen spill out. If the couple are going to cuddle together after making love, the man should wash his genitals to remove any semen that might rub off near the woman's vaginal opening.

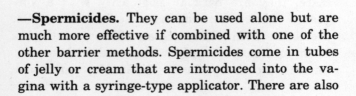

—**Spermicides.** They can be used alone but are much more effective if combined with one of the other barrier methods. Spermicides come in tubes of jelly or cream that are introduced into the vagina with a syringe-type applicator. There are also foams, and suppositories that melt into a foamy mass.

• **Natural Methods.** This is a catchall term for those methods that rely on a woman knowing, or being able to accurately calculate, when she is fertile and avoiding sex at that time. There are only about four days in each cycle when a woman can get pregnant. The ovum has a life span of twelve to twenty-four hours. The other days are accounted for by active sperm, which can live for two or three days. (So, if for example, a woman has sex on Monday, the sperm can be in her body and still alive when she ovulates on Wednesday.) Generally, a woman ovulates about fourteen days before her period starts. Unfortunately, ovulation is not related to the *previous* period, so she cannot use it to calculate when she will next ovulate. Other indications that help keep track of ovulation are the condition of the vaginal mucus and body temperature (it dips at ovulation and rises afterward). To effectively use the natural method a woman has to keep a detailed written record of her menstrual cycles for about a year. For this reason this method will not work for a young girl whose body has not settled into a regular cycle. Only the most organized and responsible adult women should attempt to use this very risky method of birth control.

CHAPTER NINE

Stories

The rest of this book contains stories that you can read to or with your daughter. They are about situations that might concern her as she sees and feels her body beginning to change during puberty.

Read the stories yourself first, and pick out those that are particularly appropriate to your daughter.

The thrust behind all the scenarios is one of open communication: to teach a girl that a sympathetic adult can do much to alleviate her anxieties and answer her questions without the fear of rejection or ridicule.

Sherri's Story

When Sherri was twelve her mom let her go to the mall for an hour after school on Fridays. Sherri went with her best friend, Holly.

They looked at all the neat clothes in the shops, went into the record store to see what new albums had arrived, and met some of the other kids at the burger stand for a soda. Then Sherri's mom picked them up and drove them home so they could get their homework done before the weekend.

One Friday, as they were going up the escalator to the second floor of the mall, Holly, who was standing behind Sherri, saw that Sherri had a small stain on her skirt. "Your period must have started," said Holly. At first Sherri was upset, then she realized it was no big deal.

Sherri took off the sweater she was wearing over her blouse and tied it around her waist. Holly told her, "It hides the stain, and it even looks cool!"

They went to the ladies' restroom and Sherri used a quarter from her soda money to buy a pad from the machine

there. Then she called her mom from a pay phone and asked her to pick them up early.

Sherri's mom said, "You acted in a very sensible way." What would you do?

Jessie's Story

When Jessie was eleven she got her first period. Her mom gave her some napkins, and told her all about how it would happen every month.

Jessie had two periods, then two months went by and she didn't get another. She didn't think much about it until she was at a slumber party one night with a bunch of girls and they started talking about their periods.

One girl, Toni, said, "You only stop getting your periods when you are going to have a baby." Jessie said hers had stopped but she couldn't be pregnant because she hadn't even been on a date with a boy!

Toni said, "You might have gotten pregnant from a toilet

seat, or from swimming in a pool with boys." Some of the other kids said they thought that was baloney, but nobody really seemed sure.

Jessie was so upset at the thought that she might be pregnant that she could hardly eat or do her schoolwork for days. She was still lying awake one night when she heard her big sister, Pam, come home from a date.

Jessie called Pam into her room and told her all about being pregnant. At first Pam thought Jessie was joking, but then she saw that her sister was crying, and realized how serious Jessie's problem was.

First Pam told Jessie that it was impossible to get pregnant from a toilet seat or from a swimming pool. "There is only one way you can get pregnant," she said, "and that is by having sexual intercourse with a boy."

Pam then explained to Jessie that it is not unusual for a girl to have irregular periods for the first year or two. "You'll probably miss quite a few periods before your body settles into its regular cycle," Pam said. "I did."

Jessie was very relieved to learn the truth. She gave Pam a big hug and they laughed together about how worried Jessie had been over nothing. Pam made Jessie promise that she would talk to her or to their mom next time she was scared about something.

What would you do?

Brooke's Story

Brooke was popular at school. She often went to different kids' homes after school to study and just hang out. When Brooke was eleven, it seemed to her that the two things they always ended up talking about were menstruating and boys.

When it came to menstruating, all the girls seemed to have heard some wild story. Charlene said, "My sister told me about this girl whose period didn't stop, so she bled to death." Another kid said, "I heard about a girl in Arizona who got a tampon stuck inside her and had to have an operation to get it out."

Brooke was pretty smart and she thought that these stories didn't sound right. She decided to ask her mom about them, even though she was kind of embarrassed to bring up the subject. Her mom couldn't help smiling when she heard some of the things Brooke's friends had been saying. She answered all of Brooke's questions and told her that the stories she had heard were not true.

When Brooke told her friends what her mom had said, some of the girls were surprised to learn that moms knew about this stuff! But they were pleased to hear the truth.

Brooke was glad she talked to her mom. What would you do?

Emma's
Story

When Emma was in the eighth grade, her class started sex education. Most of the kids laughed and joked around, especially when the teacher showed them drawings of men's and women's sex organs. Some of the boys called out crude remarks.

Emma was quite interested in seeing what everything looked like. She thought that the other kids probably were, too, but were too embarrassed to admit it. Emma couldn't really believe that she had inside her all the things that were in the women's drawing because she had never thought much about her genitals.

When she was hanging out with her friend Katherine in her bedroom after school, Emma said, "Do you think it would be really weird to look at yourself between the legs in a mirror?"

"Aagh, that's gross!" said Katherine. But after they talked about it some more, Katherine admitted that she was curious to see if she had everything in the right place. So they made a pact that that night, before they went to bed, each girl would take a hand mirror and look at herself. They agreed to tell each other the next day if they really did it.

Next day at recess, Emma and Katherine told each other
that they had looked at themselves and they had seen all the
things that were in the drawing. Now they knew much more
about their own bodies. Neither of them felt weird about it at
all, especially since each of them knew someone else had
done it too. Emma was glad she had talked to her friend
about it. What would you do?

Connie's
Story

Connie was sleeping over at her friend Rosanna's house, which she did quite often. They always had lots of fun together. They were both twelve and Rosanna's mom let them experiment with her makeup. They also made big batches of popcorn and watched rock videos.

This time Connie had her period. She had been getting it for quite a few months, but this was the first occasion she had stayed away from home overnight while she was menstruating.

Connie suddenly realized that she did not know what to do with her soiled napkins at Rosanna's house. At home, Connie, her three sisters, and her mom all put their used napkins in a little metal bin in the bathroom. Whoever was on bathroom duty that day emptied it and put in a new liner. But there wasn't a bin in the bathroom at Rosanna's house, and Connie's mom had told her not to flush napkins because they blocked the plumbing.

All through dinner Connie was very quiet because she was worrying about what to do with her pads. "What's wrong,

aren't you having a good time?" Rosanna's dad asked. Connie realized that she would not relax until she solved her problem.

When they were alone, Connie asked Rosanna what to do. "Oh, that's no problem," Rosanna said, and she told

Connie how to wrap up the napkin and place it out in the trash.

    After that, Connie was able to have fun as usual. She was pleased she had asked for information. What would you do?

Alicia's
Story

Alicia, eight, had lots of friends in the neighborhood.
They all played together in the courtyard of the apartment
block they lived in. The mother of one of the other kids looked
after them until their own parents came home from work.

One day Alicia saw a bunch of kids looking at something and laughing. She went over to them and saw that they had a magazine with a picture of a naked man in it. Alicia had never seen a man with no clothes on before. She knew that men's bodies were different from women's, but she was surprised when she saw his penis and testicles. She couldn't figure out how he went to the bathroom.

All afternoon she thought about what she had seen. When her mom came home from work that night, Alicia told

her about the picture. Alicia's mom explained to her why men and women are different, and how their bodies work.

Alicia was glad she had asked her mom. What would you do?

Joanne's
Story

Joanne was shocked. One of the kids in her class was pregnant and she was only fourteen, the same age as Joanne. Joanne didn't know the girl really well, but some of

her friends did. They talked about nothing else all day.

Carol, who knew the pregnant girl quite well, said, "She told me she only did it with her boyfriend once. She must've been lying, because you can't get pregnant the first time."

Someone else said, "She's got to be a freak—she's too young to have a baby."

When she got home, Joanne told her mom what the girls were saying. Joanne's mom explained that once a girl starts getting her periods regularly she can get pregnant the first— or any—time she has sex while she is ovulating. And it doesn't matter how old she is. Joanne didn't understand what "ovulating" meant, so her mom explained about the reproductive cycle.

Joanne felt less scared about the whole thing once her mom had explained how a girl can get pregnant. What would you do?

Dolly's Story

One summer, when Dolly was twelve, her grandpa got quite ill and Dolly's mom went to take care of him for a few weeks.

Daddy was left in charge of the family. All of the kids had jobs to do around the house. Dolly was responsible for washing up the dinner dishes and dusting the furniture. Her big brother, Andy, did the grocery shopping and kept the yard tidy.

Dolly had been menstruating for a few months, and her mom always made sure she had pads. But Dolly needed some while her mom was away, and she had run out. She

didn't want to ask Andy to get them from the store—she
knew he wouldn't want to, and he'd probably tease her.

Mom had left some money with Dolly for anything
unexpected, so Dolly decided she would buy her own pads.

She was sort of embarrassed, so she asked her friends, Rae
Lee and Chloe, to help her.

They hung around in the store for a while waiting for the
line to get short at the only lady checker. Then Dolly grabbed
a box of pads and rushed to the checkout. She was sure that
the lady was going to say something embarrassing, but she

didn't. In fact, she hardly even looked at what Dolly was buying.

When they got outside, Chloe said, "Well, that was no big deal."

"No, it wasn't," said Dolly. "Come on. I'll buy you guys some ice cream."

Dolly was proud of herself for overcoming her embarrassment. What would you do?

Tina's Story

Tina's family was very close. Every Sunday morning they would get together and talk about all kinds of things. So when Tina started menstruating, at age eleven, she told the family at their weekly meeting.

Everyone was very pleased for her. Her dad said it was a "rite of passage" and meant that she was now a woman. He said that in some cultures people celebrated when a boy or girl became an adult.

Tina's mom said, "Maybe it would be fun if we had a little celebration, too." That night she made a special dessert and they all toasted Tina with fruit punch.

Tina was very proud and happy that she could share this moment with her family.

Could you have a celebration with your family?

Morgan's Story

When Morgan, twelve, curled up in bed at night, she sometimes found that her hand tended to sneak down between her legs. She would rub herself around her clitoris and vulva. This gave her a wonderful tingly feeling.

Sometimes when she was doing it she would make up romantic stories about her favorite rock star—she would think about meeting him and kissing him! Then she would drift off to sleep.

She wondered if she was weird, but nobody knew what she was doing and it didn't seem to be doing her any harm.

Then at school one day she heard some boys teasing a
nerdy guy who wore glasses. They said he was blind
because he played with himself so much, and that he would
probably go crazy, too. Morgan felt sorry for the boy—she
thought the other kids were being mean to him. But she was
a bit worried in case what they were saying was true.

Morgan had a big brother whom she really liked. He was
home from college on vacation, and she told him what she
had heard the kids saying. Jimmy laughed and said, "All kids
play with themselves—it's called masturbating. It doesn't
make you blind or crazy or anything. As long as you don't

think about doing it so much that you stop doing other things, it can't hurt you at all."

Morgan was lucky to have a big brother to talk to. Who would you talk to?

Lori's Story

Lori, twelve, spent her summers on her uncle Matt's and aunt Zena's farm. It was something she looked forward to all year.

When Lori came back to school for seventh grade, the first thing her friend Andrea said was, "Wow, are you getting fat! They must have been feeding you well on that farm. You'd better go on a diet or you'll turn into a real blimp."

Lori was shocked. She hadn't paid too much attention to how she looked during the summer—she'd been too busy having fun with her cousins, riding horses, and helping out around the farm.

That night she looked at herself in the mirror, and sure enough, her body did look different. Her breasts were bigger and her legs and hips were definitely fatter.

So Lori started giving away her lunch, and whenever her mom put food in front of her she'd say, "Yuck, I can't eat this stuff."

After a while Lori's mom started getting worried about her. She didn't seem to be eating anything and was losing weight. One Saturday, her mom suggested she and Lori go to the country for the day. They had a really great time, and on the way home Lori started talking to her mom about being afraid of getting fat.

Her mom said, "Look at our family. Nobody in it is fat. You eat healthily and you're a very active girl. Unless you eat a lot of junk food with your friends, there is no reason why you should get fat."

She went on to explain that Lori's body was quickly changing from a little girl's to a young woman's. "You have a very nice figure," she said. "Perhaps we should buy you some more grown-up clothes; then you will see how cute you look."

Lori found out that her mom was right, and was happy that she had told her about her fears. What would you do?

Erica's
Story

Nine-year-old Erica was a bit of a tomboy. She loved roughhousing with her twin brother, Tim, and their ten-year-old cousin, David. One day they were playing with a football in the yard.

"Here, bowser breath, catch!" Tim yelled, and he threw the ball real hard to Erica. She caught it by clasping it to her chest with both arms.

"Ouch!" cried Erica, because the ball really hurt her chest on the left side. "Don't throw so hard," she said. She decided to stop playing and go inside so the boys wouldn't see that they had almost made her cry.

That night while she was putting her pajamas on, Erica noticed that her chest was still sore and was a bit puffy around her left nipple. She called for her mom and showed her the sore place.

Her mom smiled and said, "It's nothing to worry about, you are just beginning to grow up and develop breasts. The one on the right will start to grow soon, too." She explained that Erica's breasts might be a little bit tender for a while as they were growing, but that that was perfectly normal.

She also said that she would have a word with the boys about not playing so rough.

What would you do?

Reba's Story

Reba was thirteen and the only girl in her class who still hadn't gotten her period. She knew because all the girls talked about it, and some of them even started teasing her.

Reba's best friend, Marly, said, "Don't worry. My mom told me everyone starts at a different time." But Reba was still worried. She thought there might be something wrong with her, that she would never get her period. Marly said, "You should talk to your mom about it."

So finally Reba did. Her mom told her that the time a girl starts her period often runs in the family. Reba's mom told

Reba that she'd first gotten her period when she was fourteen. Reba's aunt Carol had started when she was thirteen, and Reba's grandma when she was fifteen.

"So you see," said Reba's mom, "you are quite normal

for our family. I'm sure you will start soon, as you are right on schedule in every other way."

Reba was very relieved after she had talked to her mom. What would you do?

Tricia's Story

Tricia, eleven, loved running, and since she was planning to try out for the track team she ran laps every day. After running she would pull on sweat pants and a sweater over her nylon shorts. Sometimes she would hang out with her friends for a while before she went home and changed.

Tricia soon found that she was getting very itchy around her vulva. It was really embarrassing. She wanted to scratch all the time, and she'd have to try and do it when no one was looking. When the itching didn't go away, Tricia got worried. She had heard so much about sexually transmitted diseases that she thought she had gotten one, but she didn't know how it could have happened.

The itching was particularly bad when she was running, so she started making excuses not to go to the track. Her mom guessed that something was wrong because she knew

how much Tricia loved running. Eventually, after her mom had asked her what was wrong several times, Tricia told her about the itching. Her mom said, "I'm sure it's nothing serious, but let's tell the doctor about it so we can get the problem taken care of."

The doctor did some tests and confirmed that Tricia

didn't have an infection. She said that the itching was just an irritation, and when she heard about Tricia's running, the doctor suggested that the heavy sweating, combined with hanging around in damp nylon shorts, might be the source of the problem.

Following the doctor's advice, Tricia's mom bought her some underpants and shorts made of cotton, which doesn't trap moisture against the skin as much as nylon does. Tricia started showering at the school gym and changing into clean, dry clothes after exercise. The doctor had given her some cream to stop the itching until the condition cleared up, and it cleared up very quickly after Tricia started these new habits.

She was glad she had talked to her mom instead of giving up running. What would you do?

Vanessa's Story

Vanessa used to take her baby sister, Jodi, in the bathtub with her. They splashed around together and had fun until sometimes their mom or dad had to come in and quiet them down!

One day when Vanessa was nine and Jodi was five, Jodi pointed at Vanessa and said, "What's that on you?" Vanessa looked where Jodi was pointing and saw some dark hairs growing on the area between her legs. She said, "I don't know," and tried to pull out one hair, but it hurt so much that she stopped.

Vanessa looked at herself every day. It seemed as though more hairs were growing all the time. Vanessa was getting scared because she thought something was wrong with her. Finally, she told her mom about it. "It's just a first sign that you are growing into an adult," her mom explained.

She told Vanessa some of the other things that would start to happen to her during the next few years.

Mom said that Vanessa could talk to her any time she wanted to know anything about her body. Vanessa talked to her mom lots of times after that. What would you do?

Pilar's
Story

Pilar started getting her periods when she was eleven.
She was really happy at first because she felt grown-up and
proud. Then, after about a year, she started to get cramps
every month.

They made her feel really bad for a few days. Sometimes
she would also get diarrhea and throw up. All she wanted to
do was curl up in bed with a heating pad on her stomach. But
she didn't like missing school and she hated missing drama
club.

One girl at school called her a wimp. "We all get periods too, you know. But we don't go to bed with them," she said. Pilar went home crying and told her mom what the girl had said.

Pilar's mom explained that some women have very painful cramps and that Pilar wasn't a wimp. They made an appointment for Pilar to see a gynecologist, who prescribed some medicine that helped with the pain. The doctor told Pilar that she also got bad cramps, and that sometimes it was necessary for her to lie down for a while until she felt better. Pilar was impressed; she hadn't thought of doctors getting

cramps. She didn't feel so bad now about staying in bed for a day once in a while.

Pilar was glad she told her mom how bad she felt. What would you do?

Mollie's
Story

en-year-old Mollie figured she would be getting her periods soon. Some of her friends had already started menstruating.

Mollie's mom had told her about what would happen, and Mollie was quite excited about it. She was curious about the pads she would use. One day she asked her mom if she could have a look at one of hers. Mom said she would do better than that, and would get Mollie some pads of her own, even before she needed them.

When Mollie got the package, she tore it open eagerly and examined the pads. She looked at them a number of times in the next few months. One day, without telling anyone—not even her mom or her best friend—she even wore one for a couple of hours, just to see how it felt. When Mollie got her period, she wasn't a bit concerned and knew exactly what to do.

Mollie was happy that she had asked her mom about the pads. What would you do?

Beverly's Story

Beverly's mom and dad were divorced and Beverly and her brother lived with their dad.

One day when Beverly was ten, she noticed a bloodstain on her pajama bottoms as she was getting dressed for school. Beverly was really worried. Although she had heard some kids at school talking about periods, she didn't really know what they were.

Beverly felt funny talking to her dad about it, so she went off to school without saying anything. All day she was really quiet, which was unusual for her! When Ms. Patterson

scolded her for not paying attention, Beverly just burst into tears.

Ms. Patterson asked Beverly to stay behind after class. "Now, what's really bothering you?" she asked. "You haven't been yourself today." Ms. Patterson was Beverly's favorite teacher, so she decided to tell her what was wrong.

Ms. Patterson told Beverly all about growing up, and said, "Don't worry, I'll call your dad and talk to him about

arranging for you to get everything you need."

    Beverly felt better. When she got home her dad gave her a big hug and a box of napkins. What would you do?

Gina's
Story

Gina had been looking forward to her friend Hope's birthday party for weeks. Hope was turning thirteen and having her first evening party. There was going to be pizza, fruit punch, and music to dance to. Gina's mom had even bought her a new dress.

On the morning of the party, Gina got her period. She was very upset. She thought it was going to spoil the party. "Why would you think that?" asked her mother.

Gina told her that she was afraid that she might get a stain on her new dress, or that somebody would be able to tell she had her period just by looking at her.

Mom said that first of all nobody could know she had her period unless she said something. Second, they would put an extra pad in Gina's bag along with her comb and tissues in case she needed to change at the party.

"You'll be getting a period every month for many years," her mom said. "You can't stop doing things you enjoy. All you have to do is plan to take care of it."

So Gina went to the party. None of the things she was worried about happened, and she really enjoyed herself. By the time they brought out the birthday cake she had forgotten all about her "problem." Gina was glad she had listened to her mom. What would you do?

Kim's Story

Every summer Kim went to camp for a couple of weeks. She really liked being out in the country, hiking and boating, but more than anything she loved swimming in the lake.

When she was eleven Kim started getting her periods. She didn't mind a bit, in fact she was quite proud of the fact that she was growing up.

But when it got near time for camp that year, Kim started to worry about what would happen if she got her period while she was away. She wouldn't be able to wear a bathing suit with her bulky pads, and they would show when she wore tight jeans or shorts. She started making excuses for not going to camp.

Her mom sensed that something must be wrong because she knew how much Kim enjoyed camp. "Why don't you tell me what's bothering you?" she said.

Kim blurted out her problem. Mom said the solution might be for Kim to use tampons instead of pads. She bought

Kim some junior-size tampons and explained to her how they are inserted into the vagina.

Kim was nervous about using tampons at first. But she tried them next time she got her period. At first it was a bit difficult to insert them. But with some practice, Kim was able to do it easily. By the time she went to camp, Kim was using tampons happily and didn't have to worry about going swimming.

Kim was happy she told her mom what she was worried about. What would you do?

Lisa's
Story

People sometimes called Lisa a daddy's girl, and she kind of liked that. Her mom worked long hours, and when she got home at night she was always too tired to talk to Lisa. Her dad was home much more, and he was her friend.

They cooked dinner together, and he helped her with her homework. During the weekends they would hang out together, going to the ballgame or the movies. Lisa could talk to her dad about anything—at least she thought she could.

When Lisa was ten, something embarrassing came up. All the girls in Lisa's class were wearing bras, and Lisa was developing breasts and also wanted to get a bra. But she felt really weird at the thought of talking to her dad about bras, and she just wasn't comfortable talking to her mom about personal stuff.

She felt pretty miserable—she felt like she was still a little kid! One day her grandma came for a long visit. The first

thing she said to Lisa was, "My, my, how grown-up you look You're developing quite a cute figure."

Lisa, who loved her grandma a lot, blurted out, "I think I should be wearing a bra." Then she told her grandmother all about her problem. Grandma must have told her mom and dad, because the very next Saturday Lisa's mom asked her if she'd like to go shopping for a bra. Lisa, her mom, and her grandma all went together and had fun looking at the different styles.

Her dad teased her a bit when they got home, but Lisa didn't care—she was so happy she just laughed. What would you do?

Wendy's Story

Wendy, who was eleven, and her twelve-year-old brother, Michael, got along pretty well most of the time, but occasionally they would get into a fight about something and start yelling at each other.

One day they were arguing about who did the most work around the house. Michael was being really mean to Wendy and started teasing her about the size of her breasts. She was not as well developed as some of the other girls her age.

Michael called her names like "surfboard body" and "stick woman." He shouted, "I'm going to tell Dave Martin that you only wear a training bra!"

Wendy really liked Dave, who was in her class at school. She was very upset at the thought of Michael telling Dave something personal about her.

Wendy went to her mom and told her what Michael had said. She thought her mom would just tell her to stop fighting with her brother. But to her surprise her mom said, "Don't let Michael's teasing upset you. You are just a little slow in developing, but so was I, and after a while I caught up with all my friends."

Her mom also talked to Michael in private and he stopped teasing Wendy so much.
What would you do?

Sharon's Story

Sharon was eleven. Her little sister, Debbie, was only two years younger. They lived in a big house and each girl had her own room. Ever since they'd been little they would walk in and out of each other's bedrooms without knocking.

After Sharon started getting her period, she was afraid that Debbie would burst in when she was changing and see her wearing a napkin. Sharon felt it was a private matter and she was embarrassed about anyone—even Debbie—seeing.

So even though she loved her sister, Sharon started yelling at Debbie every time she walked into Sharon's room. "Who said you could come in here?" she'd shout. Debbie would yell back and a fight would start.

Sharon's mom could tell something was wrong. "What is going on with you?" she asked Sharon. Though Sharon felt like everyone was making a lot of fuss over something personal, eventually she told her mom what was bothering her, and her mom understood exactly how Sharon felt.

Mom called Sharon and Debbie together and said, "Now that you are growing up, I think you should both knock on

each other's door before going in." Both girls agreed that they would respect each other's privacy from now on.

Sharon was glad she had talked to her mom about it. What would you do?

Heather's Story

Heather was in the sixth grade. One Monday morning she got her period, and as the day wore on she began to feel sick. She had pains in her abdomen, and she felt a little bit faint.

Heather remembered seeing an article in one of her mother's magazines about an illness called toxic shock syndrome. Women got it when they had their period, and could die from it. She started to worry that she had this disease.

She went to the school nurse and told her about it. The nurse, Mrs. Newton, told Heather, "Although some women who use tampons during their period have gotten this disease, toxic shock syndrome is *very* rare."

Mrs. Newton told Heather that the symptoms of toxic shock syndrome were a high fever, vomiting, diarrhea, a red rash, dizziness, and fainting. "I think you are having normal

menstrual cramps," she said. "Some women get them for a couple of days when they have their periods."

Mrs. Newton let Heather lie down with a heating pad on her stomach. After she'd had a nap, Heather felt much better and went to her afternoon classes.

Mrs. Newton said Heather should tell her mom about the cramps. If they got any worse, she should have a checkup, just to make sure everything was okay, and perhaps get a prescription for some painkillers.

Heather was relieved after talking to the nurse. What would you do?

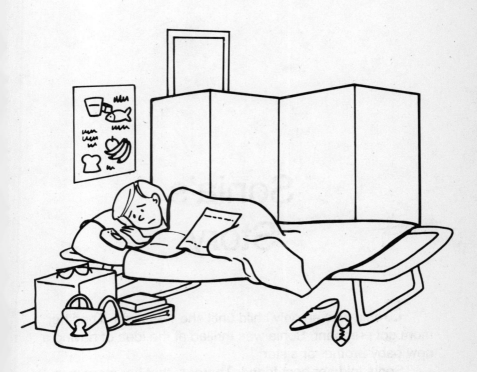

Sonia's
Story

Sonia was an only child until she was eight. Then her mom got pregnant. Sonia was thrilled at the idea of having a new baby brother or sister.

Sonia told her best friend, Theresa, that her mom was going to have a baby. Theresa said Sonia's mom and dad must have had sex. Sonia had heard some of the kids at school talking about what grown-ups do when they have sex, but she couldn't believe that her mom and dad would do things that sounded gross.

She decided to ask her mom how she had gotten pregnant, and if what Sonia had heard about sex was true.

Sonia's mom explained everything to her—all about anatomy, sex, pregnancy—anything Sonia wanted. Some of the things Sonia had heard were true, but some were completely wrong. She felt better after getting the real story from her mom, because what her mom told her didn't sound gross at all.

Sonia was relieved that her mom had cleared everything up for her. What would you do?

Pronunciation Guide

Anorexia   (ann-oh-*rex*-ee-ah)
Anus   (*ay*-nuss)
Areola   (air-ee-*oh*-lah)
Bulimia   (buh-*lee*-mee-ah)
Cervix   (*sur*-vicks)
Chlamydia   (cla-*mid*-ee-a)
Clitoris   (*clit*-or-iss)
Condom   (*con*-dum)
Depilatory   (deh-*pill*-ah-tor-ee)
Diaphragm   (*die*-a-fram)
Dysmenorrhea (dis-men-oh-*ree*-ah)
Ejaculate   (ee-*jack*-you-late)

Electrolysis	(eh-leck-*troh*-li-sis)
Endometrium	(en-doe-*mee*-tree-um)
Estrogen	(*es*-tro-gen)
Fallopian	(fa-*low*-pee-unn)
Fetus	(*fee*-tus)
Genital	(*jen*-i-t'll)
Gonorrhea	(gone-uh-*ree*-ah)
Herpes	(*her*-peas)
Hormone	(*hor*-mone)
Hymen	(*hy*-men)
Labia majora	(*lay*-bee-ah mah-*jore*-ah)
Labia minora	(*lay*-bee-ah my-*nor*-ah)
Masturbate	(*mass*-ter-bate)
Menstrual	(*men*-stral)
Menstruate	(*men*-stroo-ate)
Menstruation	(men-stroo-*ay*-shun)
Mons	(monz)
Orgasm	(*or*-gaz-um)
Ovaries	(*oh*-vah-reez)
Ovulation	(ov-you-*lay*-shun)
Ovum	(*oh*-vum)
Penis	(*pee*-nis)
Progesterone	(pro-*jes*-ta-rone)
Prostaglandin	(pros-ta-*glan*-din)
Puberty	(*pyoo*-ber-tee)
Pubic	(*pyoo*-bick)
Semen	(*see*-men)
Sperm	(spurm)
Testicles	(*tes*-ti-c'lls)
Urethra	(you-*ree*-thra)
Uterus	(*you*-ta-russ)

Vagina	(va-*jy*-na)
Vaginal	(*vaj*-i-nul)
Vaginitis	(va-ji-*ny*-tis)
Vas deferens	(vass *deh*-fa-renz)
Vulva	(*vul*-va)